THE STORY OF
Plastics

by A. A. HARNESS, A.R.I.C.

with illustrations by
B. H. ROBINSON

Publishers: Wills & Hepworth Ltd.   Loughborough
First published 1972   ©   Printed in England

Before the 'Plastics Age'.

Thousands of years ago, early men could use as materials only those things such as bones, grasses, flints and sticks that they found around them. Gradually they became more skilled in using these natural materials and, with the discovery of fire and how to use it, began to learn how to make other, more useful materials.

They found that certain clays became hard if heated in a fire, and could be used for holding water. They discovered how to make and work bronze and other metals. Slowly the range of materials they could use became greater. At the same time some men began to ask questions about the nature of the world in which they lived – and became the first *scientists*.

During the past few centuries, science has given us a much wider range of materials to use when constructing our homes and the machines which today do so much of the hard work. We no longer have to make do with what we can pick up around us. Instead we can develop special materials to meet particular needs.

If our ancestors are said to have lived in the 'Stone Age', perhaps the present time will one day be known as the 'Plastics Age'.

0 7214 0313 1

The first plastics.

The story of synthetic plastics began only a hundred years or so ago. At the Great Exhibition of 1862 at the Crystal Palace, Alexander Parkes showed a material (which he called *Parkesine*) made from cellulose nitrate. He said that this could be used for making many things – medallions, buttons, pens and penholders etc. Although Parkes worked for several years on parkesine to improve its properties, he did not develop it fully, possibly because his main interest was in the study of metals.

About the same time, a prize was offered in America for a substitute for ivory, which was in great demand for billiard balls. John Wesley Hyatt tried to win this prize, and developed a mixture of cellulose nitrate with camphor, very similar to parkesine and which he called *celluloid*. Hyatt realised the possibilities of his invention and began to develop it commercially.

The discovery and development of celluloid arose from the need to replace a scarce, natural material – ivory. Celluloid was not a perfect material – for instance, it caught fire very easily – but it *was* a new material with new properties. However, its inflammability was a serious drawback, and led to a search for a safer material with similar properties. Cellulose acetate was a promising material, and in 1894 a patent for cellulose acetate manufacture was granted to two English chemists, Cross and Bevan.

Another landmark in the history of plastics was the issuing, in America in 1907, of a patent to Leo Hendrik Baekeland. Baekeland's patent, and a similar application filed shortly afterwards in London, by Sir James Swinburne, described resins made by a chemical reaction between phenol and formaldehyde. These resins were the forerunners of the family of modern plastics known as 'thermosetting resins'.

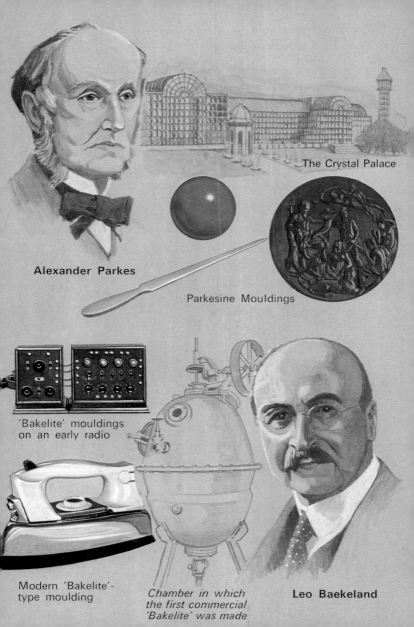

Alexander Parkes

The Crystal Palace

Parkesine Mouldings

'Bakelite' mouldings on an early radio

Modern 'Bakelite'-type moulding

Chamber in which the first commercial 'Bakelite' was made

Leo Baekeland

The importance of Cellulose Acetate.

Cellulose acetate was used in the manufacture of early aeroplanes. These machines had a wooden framework covered with cloth. The cloth was waterproofed and made to shrink tightly onto the frame by painting it with a solution of cellulose acetate in a solvent such as acetone. During the First World War large numbers of aeroplanes were built and, therefore, there was a need for large amounts of cellulose acetate. Several factories were set up to make the material.

When the war ended, the demand for aeroplanes, and for cellulose acetate, fell sharply. Not only was it plentiful and available at a reasonable price, but it also had interesting properties that had not been fully investigated.

Several research programmes were started to develop other uses for this new material. It was found possible to make clear, flexible sheets by slicing them from a large block of cellulose acetate. Early sheets made in this way were not of very good quality, and further work was carried out to develop a suitable cellulose acetate composition for this purpose. It was also discovered that artificial silks could be made from cellulose acetate.

The expansion of the cellulose acetate fibre industry led to further increases in the production of cellulose acetate. This led to an even further reduction in its price, and it could then be considered for other uses such as moulding into knife handles and similar articles.

Development of new materials.

Some plastics have been discovered almost by accident. In 1933, I.C.I. scientists at Winnington, in Cheshire, were looking at the effect of high pressures and temperatures on various materials. A gas, ethylene, was one of these. Fortunately, the ethylene contained a very small amount of oxygen which, it has since been discovered, assists the reaction which turns ethylene into polythene at the temperatures and pressures the scientists were using. When their small reactor was opened after the experiment, traces of a white, waxy, solid were found, – the first small sample of polythene.

It took a few years of work before enough polythene had been made for its properties to be fully investigated, and it was not available in quantity until the Second World War, when it was used extensively in radar installations.

Some plastics remained interesting curiosities for many years before their usefulness was appreciated. Polymethylmethacrylate was one of these, and had been known for thirty years before it became a product of commercial value. Its development was delayed because of the difficulty of making the starting material, methyl methacrylate. In 1932, chemists working in an I.C.I. laboratory discovered a way to make methyl methacrylate in quantity and at a reasonable cost. It then became possible to make polymethylmethacrylate in commercial quantities, and its toughness and transparency – in sheet form it is as clear as glass – made it suitable for applications such as aircraft canopies.

(above)   A war-time radar station
(below)   Blowing an aircraft canopy
from a plastics sheet

The development of plastics technology.

The new materials being developed required new methods to 'process' them. 'Processing' is the stage when a plastics material is moulded, or shaped, into a useful article. The development of machines designed to process plastics was slow.

At first, plastics were processed on machines designed for other purposes, and it was not until specialised machines became available that plastics could be reliably processed on a large scale.

Extrusion (squeezing heated material through a hole of the required shape – see P.40) has its origin in the spaghetti and macaroni industry, which started in Italy about 1800. In about 1850, wire was insulated with rubber and gutta-percha by a type of extrusion process. Some celluloid was extruded towards the end of the nineteenth century, but it was not until about 1930 that the extrusion of plastics became commercially important. Machines specially designed for the extrusion of plastics were not available until 1931, when Horst Heidrich designed an extruder with electrical heating and which could be fed with cold granular plastics materials.

Injection moulding (forcing just sufficient plastics material into a mould to fill it – see P.42) has its origins in machines used for die-casting of type metal, and a successful, manually-operated machine to mould plastics was developed in Germany in 1919. Ten years later, power-operated machines were being designed for use with cellulose acetate. By the time the Second World War started in 1939, some degree of automatic control had been developed.

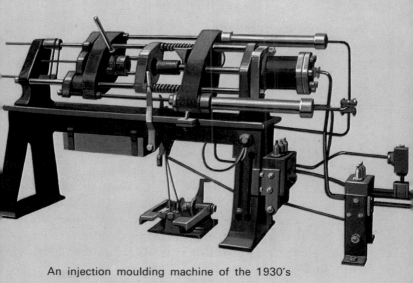

An injection moulding machine of the 1930's

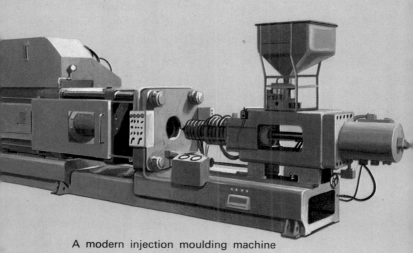

A modern injection moulding machine

War-time development.

During the Second World War, a great amount of research to develop new materials was carried out by the nations involved.

In Germany, the need became acute for materials to replace those such as rubber which were no longer available in that country. This led to the development of synthetic rubbers, considerable expansion in the production of polyvinyl chloride (PVC), and the use of polystyrene. Since Germany knew that war would break out sooner or later, this work had been in progress some years before the war actually started, and an impressive display of plastics was featured at the Düsseldorf Exhibition in 1937.

Germany developed a vigorous chemical industry based on coal. The purpose was to produce a range of hydrocarbons (compounds of carbon and hydrogen) that are the starting materials for making plastics and synthetic rubber.

In Britain it was hoped that war would be avoided and, therefore, British industry was not so well prepared when the war did break out. However, by 1940, when Germany thought she had won the war, plastics were being used in Britain in increasing quantities. Some of these replaced metals, and thus freed stocks of metal for other uses. Other plastics such as Perspex for aircraft cockpits, and *polythene* (or *polyethylene*) for insulation in radar sets, played a vital part in helping to win the war.

Understanding the new materials.

When the war ended, industry had to readjust itself and find ways of using the large quantities of new materials that factories could produce. During the war there had been a tendency to regard plastics mainly as substitutes for other materials, rather than as new materials with a place of their own in the world.

This misunderstanding of plastics continued after the war. The lack of knowledge of the properties of various plastics, together with lack of experience in their use, resulted in many badly-designed articles.

Many plastics articles made at that time were merely copies of designs which had originally been developed for use with other materials such as wood, metal and china. Such articles looked like, and indeed usually were, nasty imitations of traditional products. Many years passed before it was realised that to make the best use of modern plastics, designers had to know fully the properties of these new materials and their limitations. Design is really a combination of art and science, and must take into account the properties of the materials that are chosen for use.

In addition to bad design, there was a lack of knowledge of the best ways to fabricate plastics, and this led to many faulty products. Nowadays, the great majority of plastics articles are carefully designed and manufactured, and the old idea that plastics were substitutes for other materials is being replaced by the correct idea that plastics are new materials which have new uses.

Nylon stockings and tooth brushes, introduced during the war, were the first plastics articles to become really popular.

Unserviceable mackintoshes made from wartime P V C scrap were mainly responsible for plastics falling into disrepute during the years 1945-47.

In 1948 the first polythene bowls appeared followed by buckets. These gradually found favour with the public and pioneered the way for other household articles in plastics.

By 1960 plastics articles were widely accepted by the public and largely replaced the traditional enamelled and galvanised, iron hollow-ware over which they had obvious advantages.

What are plastics?

Many substances which we use today are *chemical compounds*. Salt is a compound of sodium and chlorine, sugar is a compound of carbon, hydrogen and oxygen. Sodium, chlorine, carbon, hydrogen and oxygen are examples of *elements*. No matter how hard we try, we cannot break up an element into any simpler chemicals.

The smallest particle of an element that can exist is an atom. When two or more atoms are joined together, we call this a molecule. A molecule of cane sugar contains 12 atoms of carbon, 11 of oxygen and 22 of hydrogen. Sugar is one of the larger molecules among common materials.

Carbon atoms have an important chemical property: they can join together to form long chains. Other atoms—hydrogen, oxygen, nitrogen, chlorine or more carbon atoms, for instance, can be joined to the carbon atoms in such chains to make very large molecules. Life, as we know it, could not exist if it were not for this extraordinary property of carbon, since most of the compounds found in plants and animals are made in this way.

What has all this to do with plastics? Quite simply, most of the plastics we find around us today are compounds made with long chains of carbon atoms. It is these long chains that give plastics the properties that we find so useful.

An oxygen atom   A hydrogen atom   A carbon atom

One oxygen and two hydrogen atoms combined to form a water molecule

A Molecule of Cane Sugar

The essential linking of the molecules.

Let us look at one of the common plastics – *polythene*, for example. Polythene is a tough, solid material. Ethylene, from which it is made, is a gas. A molecule of polythene is made by persuading lots of molecules of ethylene to join together. Many hundreds – even thousands – of ethylene molecules must be joined together to make a molecule of polythene. Small molecules such as ethylene, which can link together in this way, are called *monomers*. The process of joining the molecules together is known as *polymerisation*. The large molecules, such as polythene, which are thus formed are called *polymers*.

Imagine all the children in a school running around in the playground, darting here and there, each going his or her own way. This is how molecules of a gas, such as ethylene, behave.

Now imagine that the children start to link arms together; first two join together, then a third joins them, then a fourth and so on until we have a long chain of children. They are now like a molecule of polythene. Imagine many lines of children all tangled up together. This is a rough picture of the way the molecules exist in a piece of polythene.

Ethylene molecules will not link up together without persuasion. Chemicals known as *catalysts*, or *initiators*, have to be used to provide this persuasion and start the process off. One of the jobs of polymer chemists is to find out the best conditions for this polymerisation, or linking together of small molecules, to take place.

All synthetic plastics are made by joining together small molecules to make very big ones, (big, that is, for molecules. It takes a few hundred polythene molecules joined end to end to stretch even one millimetre).

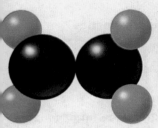

*Ethylene molecule
(2 carbon atoms,
4 hydrogen atoms)*

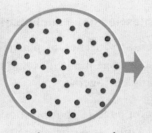

*Arrangement of
molecules*

GAS

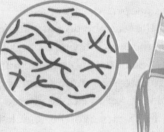

LIQUID

*With the addition of a catalyst the molecules
join together and begin to form chains*

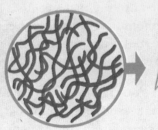

SOLID

*When polymerisation is complete the long chains
are tangled together, forming polythene*

Why do plastics have such useful properties?

The useful properties of plastics arise from the presence of these large molecules and the way in which they become tangled together.

We saw on page 18 that plastics are made up of long, chain molecules. It is the existence of these long chains that makes plastics different from other chemical compounds.

The researches of chemists and physicists have shown that the properties of a plastics material do not depend *only* on the way the polymer molecules are built up, but also on the way they are tangled together in the solid material. Scientists now understand plastics well enough to be able to say, quite often, how the properties of a particular material can be altered or improved. Whereas twenty-five years ago the search for new plastics was a rather hit-or-miss affair, today research workers have a fairly good idea of how to set about making a plastic with certain required properties.

This is not to say that scientists know all that there is to know about the relations between molecular structure and properties. Far from it; there is still a lot to be done and learned.

To carry out this research involves the use of complicated and expensive equipment, and occupies many talented scientists and their teams of assistants.

Exploratory research leading to a new plastic

The raw material for plastics.

If you were asked to name the most important raw materials used today, your list would certainly include oil. Oil is used to provide much of our heat and power, and it is also the raw material from which many chemical products are manufactured, including those used to make plastics.

The oil deposits which we use today have taken millions of years to form. Long before the first men appeared, the earth was covered by warm, shallow seas. These seas provided ideal conditions for the millions of tiny sea animals which lived and died in them. When the creatures died, they sank to the bottom of the seas and their remains helped to build up a layer of sludge.

As time went by, and under the pressure caused by the weight of mud and other deposits above them, the remains of these tiny creatures slowly changed into oil. The mud gradually hardened into a porous rock, and the droplets of oil soaked into, and spread through, this porous rock. In this way, it is believed, were formed the oilfields from which we get our oil today. Some of these oilfields are still under the sea, though in other places the seas have dried up since the oilfields were formed, leaving the oil buried under dry land.

When it comes from the oil wells, the oil has to be separated into its various components. This is carried out by a process known as *distillation*. In this process the oil is heated so that the various components, or *fractions*, which boil at different temperatures, are boiled out of the crude oil, one after another. When each boils, its vapours are condensed back into liquids, and separately collected from the distillation column.

The remains of tiny animals and plants accumulated at the bottom of shallow seas.

Cross-section of an oilfield. Pressures cause the oil to move upwards between the rock grains, to form a reservoir beneath the 'cap' of impervious rock.

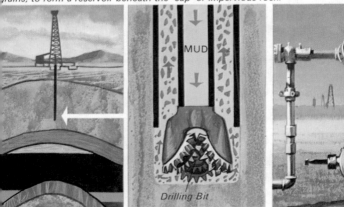

Drilling for oil. Mud is pumped through the drill pipe and back to the surface bringing with it the fragments of drilled rock.

A Well head. A set of valves controls the flow of oil.

Oil distillation provides the raw materials for plastics.

Distillation, as carried out in an oil refinery is, of course, much more complex than in the simple description on the last page. The fractions with the lower boiling points, known as *light fractions*, are used for making petrols and similar fuels. The other materials with higher boiling points, (*heavy fractions*) are taken and, in a term used by the oil industry, are *cracked* to convert them into simpler chemicals. To a large extent the *cracking* can be controlled to produce some materials in greater quantities than others. In this way, the chemicals used as raw materials *(feedstocks)* by the plastics industry are obtained.

One of these chemicals is ethylene, which is not only made directly into polythene but is also converted into other chemicals used in making plastics. Other chemicals obtained include propylene and also butadiene, which is used for making some synthetic rubbers. Sometimes chemicals from other sources are used, as in the manufacture of vinyl chloride. For this, chlorine is needed and it is obtained from common salt (sodium chloride).

The raw materials of the plastics industry are mainly oil, air, salt and water, but many different chemical processes are involved before these are converted into plastics.

In the production of some plastics such as nylon, ammonia is needed. Nitrogen is obtained from the air and is used to make the ammonia.

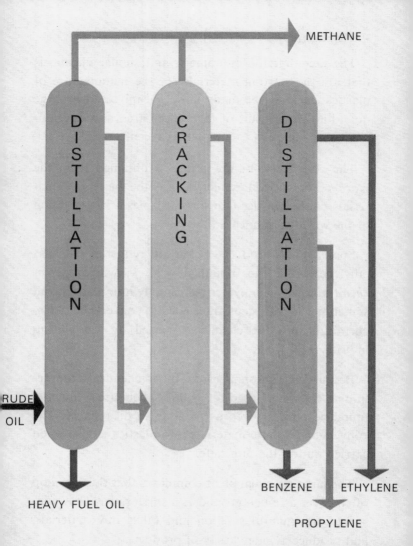

METHANE

DISTILLATION

CRACKING

DISTILLATION

CRUDE OIL

HEAVY FUEL OIL

BENZENE

PROPYLENE

ETHYLENE

Raw materials for plastics

RAW MATERIALS FOR PLASTICS FROM
CRUDE OIL

Petrochemicals.

The fact that the monomers, and similar chemicals that are the starting materials for the manufacture of plastics, can now be made fairly cheaply, and in large quantities, is a result of all the research and development that has been carried out in recent years.

The conversion of the products obtained from the *crackers* of the oil refineries into the basic raw materials of the plastics industry, occupies a large section of the world's chemical industry.

Some of the products of the oil refineries (such as ethylene, propylene, butadiene – all known as *petrochemicals*) can be polymerised directly into plastics, but sometimes several steps are needed to convert the petrochemicals into the chemicals needed by the plastics industry.

Because large tonnages of these chemicals are required, the plants used for making them are frequently found next to, or even as part of, an oil refinery. The conversion of these materials into plastics is also often carried out on the same site.

The large chemical plant complexes that thus develop often cover as much ground as a small town. They consume vast quantities of oil and other raw materials, and produce a wide variety of products.

Part of the polymerisation building at a large chemical plant

The making of PVC.

Chemists have developed a number of different polymerisation systems (the linking together of molecules), some being suitable for making a variety of plastics, others having been developed to make particular products.

One polymerisation system with wide applications is that in which the monomer, in the form of bubbles or droplets, is kept suspended in water by stirring during polymerisation. The separation of the monomer droplets in the water is assisted by adding a small quantity of a chemical, similar to a soap or detergent, called an *emulsifying agent*.

Hundreds of thousands of tons of PVC are made in this way every year. A large vessel, called an *autoclave*, which can withstand pressures of up to 200 lb/in^2 (14 kg/cm^2), is partly filled with water containing small amounts of catalyst and emulsifying agent. An amount of vinyl chloride, roughly equal in volume to the water, is added and stirred until it is broken into small droplets suspended in the water. The autoclave, and its contents, are then heated to about 50°C and the vinyl chloride droplets polymerise to form solid particles of PVC. These remain suspended in the water, forming a milky emulsion, or latex. The emulsion is cooled and then run out of the autoclave. Sometimes it is used as an emulsion, but more often it is dried and a fine powdery form of PVC obtained.

The autoclave section of a PVC plant

The making of Perspex and Polythene.

An example of a quite different process, which has been developed to make a particular product, is that for making acrylic sheet material such as *Perspex.

Perspex is made by polymerising methyl methacrylate in a cell constructed from two sheets of glass separated by a rubber ring (or gasket). In practice, the methyl methacrylate is partly polymerised, becoming thick and syrupy, before it is put into the cell. The polymerisation is completed by heating the filled cell in an oven. When the polymerisation is complete, the cell is cooled and the glass plates removed, leaving a sheet of clear, solid, polymethyl methacrylate – Perspex.

Another quite different method of making a polymer is the process developed by I.C.I. for the manufacture of polythene, and which involves the use of very high pressures and quite high temperatures. In this process the monomer, ethylene gas, is compressed to a pressure of over 15,000 lb/in² (100 kg/cm²) and, with a catalyst, is fed into a special reactor designed to withstand these pressures. In the reactor, at a temperature between 150° and 250°C, the compressed ethylene polymerises to form polythene, which is forced out as a molten stream, through a special valve at the bottom of the reactor. It is then cooled and cut into small granules.

There are many other ways in which polymers are made. For instance, nylon polymers are made by heating two chemicals together, so that the long chain molecules are built from bits of each reactant alternately.

* *Perspex is a trade mark of Imperial Chemical Industries Limited.*

The control room of a plastics plant

Thermoplastics and thermosetting materials.

Plastics materials can be divided broadly into two classes, *thermoplastic* and *thermosetting*. The first of these, which includes common plastics such as polythene, PVC and polystyrene, are materials which can be softened by heating, and which harden again on cooling. This process of softening and hardening by heating and cooling, can be repeated over and over again. Thermosetting materials, on the other hand, first soften on heating and then, with further heating, set hard and afterwards cannot be softened again by heat – just like the white of an egg which changes to a firm solid when it is cooked. An example of such a plastic is the 'bakelite' type of material used for saucepan handles, etc.

What is the difference – chemically – between these two classes of plastics materials? We have already seen (P.18) that plastics are chemical compounds that have very long molecules. In thermoplastic materials, these long molecules are separate from each other. In thermosetting materials, heating causes strong chemical links to be formed *between* the long molecules, thus joining them firmly together.

This joining together of long chain molecules is called *cross linking* and it is this kind of reaction between the protein molecules of an egg that causes it to solidify when it is cooked.

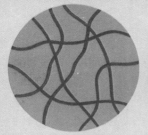

In a THERMOPLASTIC material the chains of molecules are entangled and hold each other in place

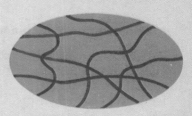

When heated the chains slide over each other and the plastic can be forced into a new shape

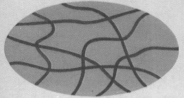

When cool the thermoplastic retains its new shape

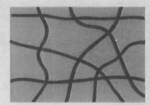

When reheated it can be forced into a different shape

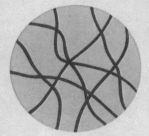

A THERMOSETTING material, likewise, can be forced into a new shape when heated

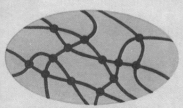

But as heating continues links are formed where the chains cross each other

The links are permanent and its shape cannot be changed by reheating or by force

Making things from plastics.

Polymers are usually mixed with other materials which alter their properties. For example, small amounts of special chemicals are added to make the material less liable to damage by oxygen in the air, or by strong sunlight. Dyes or pigments are added to give colour to the finished articles. *Plasticisers*, which are usually oily liquids, may be added to make the material softer. *Fillers*, such as chalk or glass fibre, may be added to make it stiffer.

A polythene bowl contains pigment to give it colour, and chemicals to stop oxidation: PVC wire-covering contains pigment to give it colour, chemicals to stop oxidation and plasticiser to make it flexible; a thermoset moulding contains pigment to give it colour and a filler to make it less brittle.

Both thermoplastics and thermosetting resins require heat as well as pressure to shape them into useful articles. However, as we have read, thermosetting materials cannot be remelted and made into another shape. Most things made from thermosetting materials are made by forcing the material into the desired shape by heat and pressure, and then keeping it hot until it has set or *cured*. A hydraulic press is often used to provide the pressure, with moulds heated by steam or electricity.

The right amount of thermosetting plastic is put into a hot mould in the press (illustration and Fig. 1) and the mould is closed. The plastic gets hot, softens, flows under the pressure so as to fill the mould and take its shape, and then hardens (Fig. 2). The mould is opened, the hot moulding is taken out and the process starts all over again (Fig. 3).

Making a tray from thermosetting plastic

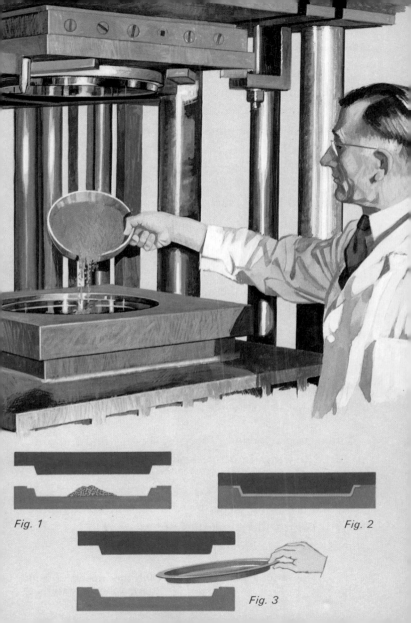

Fig. 1

Fig. 2

Fig. 3

More about making things from plastics.

All the steps mentioned on the previous page can be carried out automatically on specially designed presses. Once the press and moulds have been set up and the process started, mouldings can be made continuously. Small things like bottle caps can be made at the rate of several a minute, whilst larger items take a little longer.

Laminated boards, such as those used to make working surfaces in kitchens, are made by pressing a thermosetting resin into layers of paper or cloth between heated flat plates.

As we have read, thermoplastics can be softened by heating, and must be allowed to cool so that they become hard enough to keep their shape. Processing of thermoplastics, therefore, involves three stages, whatever method is used. The material is first heated enough to soften it, then it is forced into the desired shape, and lastly it is left to cool while it is still held in its new shape.

Often, in production processes, stages 1 and 2 appear to blend together into one heating and shaping operation.

In the following pages we will look at some of the ways in which thermoplastics are made into everyday things.

The various stages of processing thermosetting and thermoplastic materials

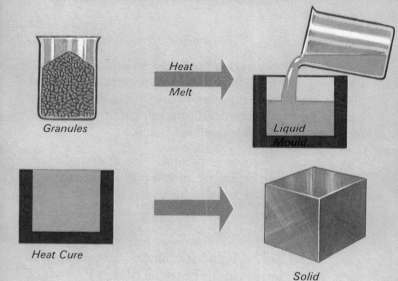

Heat
Melt

Granules

Liquid
Mould

Heat Cure

Solid

THERMOSETTING MATERIALS

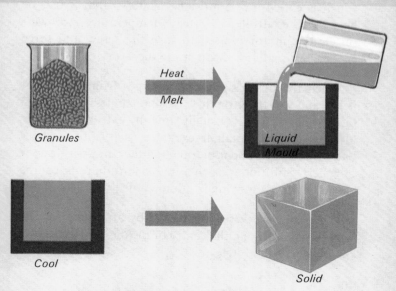

Heat
Melt

Granules

Liquid
Mould

Cool

Solid

THERMOPLASTIC MATERIALS

Extrusion.

This is the process that is used to make things such as PVC and polythene pipes and nylon curtain rails, and also to cover wire with plastics insulation. It consists of heating the plastics material, squeezing it through a hole of the right shape, and then cooling it.

A household mincer is a simple type of extruder. It has a hopper into which the meat is put, a screw to push the meat along, and holes at the end through which the meat is forced.

An extruder designed to work with plastics is basically a larger and more complicated mincer. Because plastics need heat to soften them, the barrel (that is the part of an extruder between the hopper and the hole at the end, which is called a *die*) must be made so that it can be heated and controlled at a steady temperature. A powerful electric motor is used to turn the screw and force the plastics material through the die.

When the plastics material emerges from the die, it is hot and will therefore lose its shape unless it is cooled fairly quickly. This is usually done by extruding flexible articles, such as draught excluder strip, into a water bath and pulling them out at the other end with a pair of rollers. Stiff things, such as nylon curtain rails, can be extruded onto a moving belt and cooled with jets of air.

Wire can be covered with PVC by arranging for the wire to pass through the centre of the die, and extruding the plastic around it.

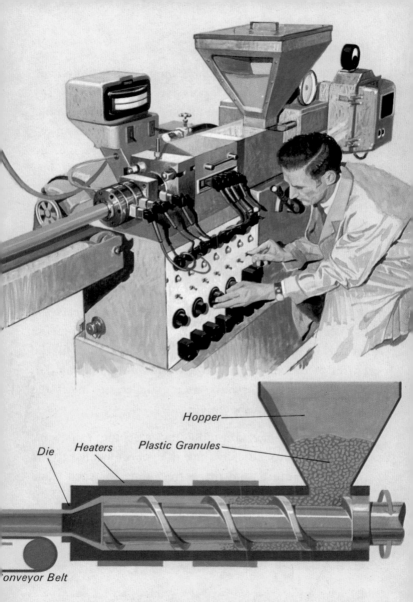

Hopper

Plastic Granules

Die

Heaters

Conveyor Belt

SIMPLIFIED CROSS-SECTION OF AN EXTRUDER

Injection moulding.

This process is used to make things such as polythene bowls, nylon gear wheels, polystyrene cases for transistor radios, etc. Injection moulding machines are similar in some ways to extruders, except that whereas an extruder continually forces material through a die, an injection moulding machine is designed to force just sufficient plastics material into a cool mould to fill it. It then waits until the moulded article has cooled, and been removed from the mould, before filling the mould again.

Some smaller machines use a simple plunger to push the material from the hot barrel into the mould. Larger machines use a screw, which first mixes and heats the plastics material thoroughly, before forcing it into the mould. In these machines, the screw is rotated to fill the barrel of the machine with a fresh charge of material, and then moves forward, as a plunger, to inject the molten plastic into the mould.

A modern, injection-moulding machine can work completely automatically once it has been heated to the right temperature, and the correct time for each stage (mould filling, cooling of moulding and removal of moulding) set on the controls.

Since the process is automatic, it is particularly useful when large numbers of identical mouldings are needed.

Heaters

Mould

Screw Plunger

SIMPLIFIED CROSS-SECTION OF AN INJECTION
MOULDING MACHINE

Thermo-forming.

Some plastics articles are made by heating and shaping a piece of thermoplastic sheet which has previously been made by extrusion, or by *calendering*, (when softened plastics material is squeezed between hot metal rollers), or has been polymerised as a sheet (P.32).

The sheet is cut to a suitable size, heated until it is soft and rubbery and then forced into, or onto, a mould to give it the desired shape. When the shaped article has cooled and hardened, it is removed from the mould and the edges of the article are trimmed off.

The pressure needed to shape the softened sheet can be applied in any one of three main ways. Compressed air can be used to blow the sheet into shape, or the sheet can be sucked into a mould by a vacuum, or a plunger or ram can force the sheet into the desired shape. Sometimes a combination of these methods is used. For example, when making a deep article such as a bath, a mechanical ram can be used to push the hot sheet into the mould, and vacuum applied to complete the shaping.

Other examples of things made from sheet are chocolate box trays which are vacuum-formed from thin sheet; illuminated signs, which are sometimes made from several shaped pieces cemented together; and windshields for motor scooters. Plastic bottles are made by a process called 'extrusion blow moulding' which really combines extrusion with thermo-forming. The bottle is blown into shape from a length of hot tube, which is usually extruded directly into the mould.

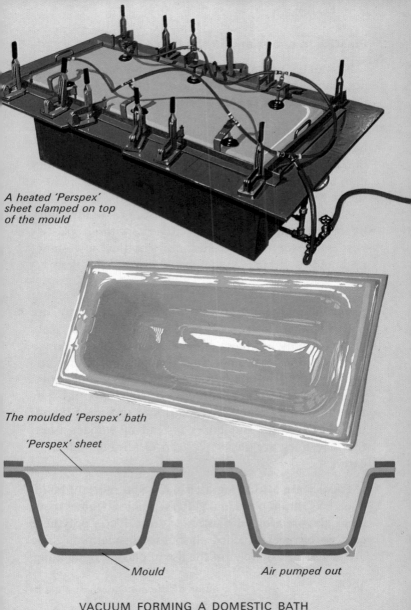

A heated 'Perspex' sheet clamped on top of the mould

The moulded 'Perspex' bath

'Perspex' sheet

Mould

Air pumped out

VACUUM FORMING A DOMESTIC BATH

Plastics in shops and in the home.

Nowadays we take plastics for granted, and we do not realise that not very long ago the number of plastics things we used in our daily lives were very few.

Imagine life now without polythene bowls and buckets which do not rust or scratch sinks; without PVC tiles and floor covering for kitchens and shops; without illuminated road and shop signs made from plastics sheet; without polythene bags for wrapping goods from apples to zip fasteners; without plastics cases for things like electric mixers and hair dryers; without plastics bottles for everything – from squeezy bottles for washing-up liquid to attractively-designed cosmetics bottles.

In many ways plastics help to make life easier, more colourful and even quieter. Most dairies today use plastics crates, instead of the wire ones of a few years ago. Not only are these crates lighter for the milkman to handle, but we are not wakened early in the morning by the rattling of milk bottles against their metal crates. Plastics crates are not only used by dairies but also by most industries which have bottles to transport. Shops use plastics trays and boxes instead of wooden ones; the new ones are easier to keep clean and lighter to carry.

Plastics are also being used more and more in buildings; PVC drain pipes and gutters; window frames made from glass-reinforced plastics or from PVC; polythene cold water pipes; foamed plastics for insulation – these are just some examples of the use of plastics in building.

Stacking chairs in glass fibre reinforced nylon

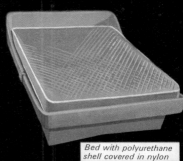

Bed with polyurethane shell covered in nylon

Trousers, suit and boots in PVC

Containers and bottles in polythene

Vinyl floor tiles

Clock in 'Perspex'

Corrugated PVC sheets

Bottle crate in 'Propathene'

Plastics in transport and engineering.

Today, plastics are widely used in the home, but they have many other uses which are less obvious, but nevertheless important, in engineering, in transport and in the electrical industry.

Nylon gear wheels have replaced metal ones in many instances. In machines used on farms, for example, nylon gear wheels last longer than steel ones because they work without needing oil and do not rust.

Because of its great slipperiness, PTFE (most commonly-known as the non-stick coating on pans) is used for bearings which it is difficult or undesirable to lubricate. One interesting use for PTFE is in bridge construction. In many new bridges, the ends move on pads of PTFE as the sections of bridge expand or contract with changes in temperature. (See illustration opposite.)

In the electrical industry, the advantages of plastics such as polythene and PVC have made possible the design and use of equipment that is superior to that which would have been possible without them. Nylon is also used in electrical equipment, its combination of strength and stiffness with good insulating properties making it particularly valuable, for example, in the bodies of power tools. Some of the uses of plastics in cars are obvious, such as materials for seats and lenses for lights. Some are less obvious – such as ducting for ventilation systems, insulation for electrical parts, etc.

Plastics are indeed an important part of our world, not only in our homes but also when they quietly perform some essential purpose, tucked away and out of sight.

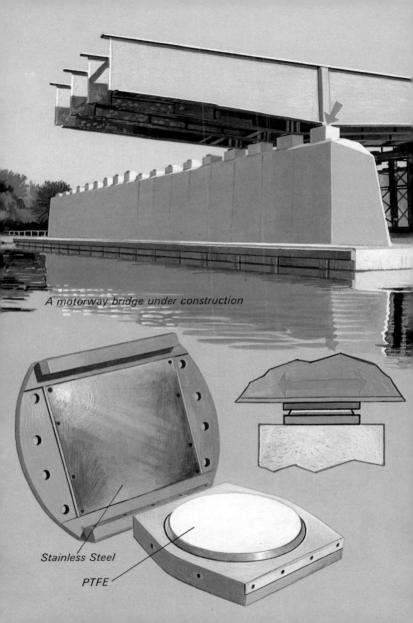

A motorway bridge under construction

Stainless Steel

PTFE

The future of plastics.

The use of plastics of all types is increasing, and will almost certainly continue to increase. The development of existing plastics, and possibly the discovery of new materials, will mean that in the future plastics will be used for even more purposes than they are today.

For instance, by using carbon fibres instead of glass fibres to reinforce plastics materials, we can obtain products with greater strength and rigidity. No doubt chemists will develop new resins to make even better use of the properties of carbon fibres.

The development of rockets, and of space travel, have given scientists the spur to seek new lightweight materials that will be suitable for use at high temperatures. Possibly some of these materials will be new plastics, and their development could mean even further widespread use of plastics.

It has been estimated that within fifteen years the total volume of plastics used will equal the total volume of metals used. Perhaps we might guess that plastics will be used more and more in building, in transport and in machinery of all kinds, and we will probably be right. It would not be wise, however, to try to guess the purposes for which plastics will *not* be used fifteen years from now!

Glossary of Terms

ATOM   The smallest particle of an element.

CATALYST or INITIATOR   A chemical which persuades molecules to link together.

CRACKING   The conversion of fractions into simpler chemicals.

ELEMENT   A substance which cannot be broken down into other chemicals.

EXTRUSION   Squeezing heated material through a hole of the required shape.

FRACTIONS   The various components of crude oil.

INJECTION MOULDING   Forcing just sufficient plastics material into a mould to fill it.

MONOMERS   Small molecules which can link together.

POLYMERS   Large molecules formed when small molecules (monomers) link together.

POLYMERIZATION   The process of linking small molecules together to form chains.

PROCESSING   The stage when a plastics material is moulded or shaped into a useful article.

Contents

	Page
Before the 'Plastics Age'	4
The first plastics	6
The importance of Cellulose Acetate	8
Development of new materials	10
The development of plastics technology	12
War-time development	14
Understanding the new materials	16
What are plastics?	18
The essential linking of the molecules	20
Why do plastics have such useful properties?	22
The raw material for plastics	24
Oil distillation provides the raw materials for plastics	26
Petrochemicals	28
The making of PVC	30
The making of Perspex and Polythene	32
Thermoplastics and thermosetting materials	34
Making things from plastics	36
More about making things from plastics	38
Extrusion	40
Injection moulding	42
Thermo-forming	44
Plastics in shops and in the home	46
Plastics in transport and engineering	48
The future of plastics	50